Who Pooped in the Park?

Written by Gary D. Robson
Illustrated by Robert Rath

FARCOUNTRY
PRESS

To my big brother Neil, the desert expert.
-Gary

For Lucy and Thomas, my poop experts.
-Robert

ISBN 1-56037-371-7

© 2006 Farcountry Press
Text © 2006 Gary D. Robson
Illustrations © 2006 Farcountry Press

For more information on our books,
write Farcountry Press, P.O. Box 5630, Helena, MT 59604;
call (800) 821-3874; or visit www.farcountrypress.com.

Book design by Robert Rath.
Created, produced, and designed in the United States.
Printed in China.

10 09 08 07 06 05   1 2 3 4 5 6

Library of Congress Cataloging-in-Publication Data

Robson, Gary D.
   Who pooped in the park?. Red Rock Canyon National Conservation Area / [Gary D Robson and Robert Rath].
      p. cm.
   ISBN-13: 978-1-56037-371-1
   1. Animal tracks—Nevada—Red Rock Canyon National Conservation Area—Juvenile literature. I. Rath, Robert. II. Title.
   QL768.R63 2005
   591.9794'88—dc22
                    2005013403

"Dad? I have to go to the bathroom." Michael squirmed in the back seat.

"We'll be at our campground in just a little while," said Dad. "We're entering the Red Rock Canyon National Conservation Area now."

"He's just nervous," said Michael's sister. "He thinks a mountain lion's gonna eat him." She growled at Michael and made her fingers look like claws.

"Stop it, Emily," said Mom. "Nobody is getting eaten by anything."

4

Michael was very excited about the trip, but Emily was right. He *was* nervous. He had just read a book about big cats, and mountain lions were scary!

He was afraid that a hungry mountain lion would eat just about anything—maybe even a boy.

5

"I *am* kind of scared of mountain lions," admitted Michael.

"Don't worry," Dad told him. "Mountain lions tend to stay away from people. Besides, we're going to show you how to learn all about them without ever getting close!"

"Here's our campsite. Let's set up the tent. Then we can go for a walk and I'll show you what I mean," Dad said.

Michael was awfully worried about mountain lions, but tried not to show it.

"Let's hurry!" said Emily. "I want to see some animals!"

Once the tent was up, the whole family went to the Visitor Center.

"Look at this big turtle," said Michael. "Where's its pond?"

"That's a desert tortoise," Dad answered. "They don't live in ponds."

"Are there more of them?" asked Emily, looking around.

the STRAIGHT POOP

The desert tortoise is Nevada's state reptile. They are endangered, and it's against the law to bother or catch them.

"There are lots around here. But when it gets hot, they go into their burrows," said Mom. "So we'll need to look for their *sign*."

"Sign?" said Michael. "You mean like a sign at the zoo?"

GREAT HORNED OWL

BURRO

COYOTE

9

"By the word 'sign,' I mean a clue that an animal has been around," Mom said. "See the hole in the ground there? That's the entrance to a tortoise's burrow, and you can see its tracks there, too."

the STRAIGHT POOP

Desert tortoises sometimes share their burrows with snakes. They don't bother each other.

The STRAIGHT POOP

The northern flicker is a woodpecker that often makes holes in cactus plants and nests in them.

"And over here, you can see where it was eating these desert grasses," Dad added.

"And pooping, too," giggled Michael.

"Trackers and hikers call it 'scat' instead of poop," said Mom with a smile.

"See, Michael," said Dad. "We don't have to get up close to an animal to learn about it. Instead of a close encounter of the *scary* kind, we'll have a close encounter of the *poopy* kind."

Everybody laughed, and Mom made a gross-out face.

"Let's see if we can find some more animals," said Emily.

"I'm going to find more scat," said Michael, trying to sound grown up.

13

"Dad! Mom! Look over here! I found bunny scat!" yelled Michael. "It's just like what we have in Fluffy's cage at home."

"We came all the way here for *that*?" grumbled Emily. "Michael's bunny makes plenty of poop at home."

the STRAIGHT POOP

Rabbits eat their own scat! They do this to get as much nutrition from the food as they can. The little brown balls are scat that's already been through twice.

Black-tailed jackrabbits can leap up to ten feet in a single bound.

"Where is the rabbit?" asked Michael.

"It looks like it took off in a hurry," Dad answered. "Look how far apart these tracks are! It must have been a jackrabbit."

"I'll bet the jackrabbit was running from a snake," Mom added. "See the marks by Michael's feet?"

Emily was starting to get interested. "Can we follow the tracks and try to find them?"

the STRAIGHT POOP

Stay away from rattlesnakes! Most snakes are harmless, but Mojave green rattlesnakes have a deadly bite.

"Definitely not," said Mom. "There's a type of rattlesnake here called a Mojave green. They're very dangerous, and we don't want to find one."

the STRAIGHT POOP

Despite the name, jackrabbits aren't really rabbits, they're hares. Hares usually have bigger ears and back legs than rabbits, and they can run much faster.

A little farther along, Emily spotted more tracks by the rocks. "These are funny looking," she said. "Are they from a rabbit, too?"

"Let's take a look," said Dad. "The back foot shows five toes, and they look different from rabbit toes. I think these are rodent tracks."

the STRAIGHT POOP

Rodents are small gnawing animals such as mice, rats, hamsters, and squirrels.

the STRAIGHT POOP

Pack rats, also called woodrats, like to line their nests with shiny objects.

"I'd say it's a pack rat," said Mom. "And here's its nest!"

"Do pack rats really steal things and leave other stuff to pay for it?" asked Emily, remembering a show she had seen on TV.

"Pack rats really like shiny things," answered Mom. "They can only carry one object at a time, so if they see something shiny, they'll drop what they're carrying and pick up the shiny thing instead. It does kind of seem like the pack rats are paying for it."

"Emily collects shiny stuff. Is she a pack rat?" Michael smiled.

Emily giggled and stuck out her tongue at him.

the STRAIGHT POOP

When pack rats pee in their nests, their collections harden into something called a "midden." Scientists learn about the way things used to be by studying fossilized pack rat middens that are tens of thousands of years old.

Near the pack rat nest, Michael spotted something else. "I found some big scat!" he said. "And some tracks."

He looked around nervously. "This isn't from a mountain lion, is it?"

Dad replied, "Don't worry, Michael, this is coyote sign."

"They look like dog tracks," said Emily.

"That's because coyotes are in the dog family," explained Dad.

the STRAIGHT POOP

You can tell what a coyote has been eating by looking at its scat. Coyote scat often has hair and bits of bones in it that their bodies can't digest—that's how you can tell coyote poop from dog poop.

"I'll bet the coyote was hanging out here looking for a meal," said Mom.

"It wanted to eat the pack rat?" asked Emily.

"Yep, a pack rat, roadrunner, or other small creature. Coyotes will eat anything they can catch," answered Mom.

"That's why the pack rat's nest has sharp, spiny stuff all around the entrance. It's trying to stay out of reach of coyotes and other animals," added Dad.

23

"Let's head up this way," said Dad. "We can see more of the scenery from over there."

"These red rocks are beautiful," said Emily.

"Yes, they are," agreed Mom. They were formed hundreds of millions of years ago, when this was the bottom of an ocean."

"More scat!" yelled Michael. "And this stuff is even *bigger*! Is it from a big mountain lion?" He tried not to get scared.

"That's from a burro," said Dad.

Michael was very relieved.

Dad said, "See how the hoof-prints look just like the ones from a horse, only smaller?"

"There are wild horses out here, too," added Mom.

the STRAIGHT POOP

It's easy to tell a burro from a horse: a burro is smaller and has a white muzzle, black edges around its ears, and black fur in the shape of a cross on its shoulders.

the STRAIGHT
POOP

Horses and burros can
poop while they walk,
but they have to stop to pee.

"Horses and burros were brought
to America hundreds of years
ago by early settlers. Many got
away and formed wild herds,"
Mom told the kids.

"Look at that huge lizard!" said Michael.

"It's a chuckwalla," Dad answered. "They're not dangerous, but you shouldn't bother them."

"You shouldn't touch the plants, either," Mom added. "Banana yuccas are beautiful, but the leaves have sharp edges."

the STRAIGHT POOP

The banana yucca was popular with Native Americans. They made soap from the roots and string from the leaves.

"Is this bird poop?" said Michael, looking at a nearby Joshua tree.

"Yes," said Mom. "Those white streaks on the tree are owl scat. See these tracks with two toes pointing forward and two pointing back, and the owl pellets around the base of the tree?"

"Owl pellets?" said Emily.

"Owls eat their prey whole," explained Mom. "The parts they can't digest, like hair and bones, get coughed up in a pellet like this."

the STRAIGHT POOP

Studying owl pellets is a great way to find out what owls eat. They dine on small animals such as mice, birds, and lizards.

"Yuck!" said Emily.

"You can tell this was a big owl by the size of the tracks and the pellets," said Mom. "The bigger the owl, the bigger the owl pellets."

"There are a bunch of different owls in Red Rock Canyon," said Dad. "My favorite is the great horned owl."

Michael had forgotten about mountain lions and was hunting for more scat. "Is this more bunny poop?" he asked.

Dad took a closer look. "This is bigger than rabbit scat. You've found the scat of a desert bighorn sheep."

RABBIT SCAT

"Rabbit scat looks like little brown balls," Dad continued, "but bighorn sheep scat is shaped more like jellybeans."

BIGHORN SHEEP SCAT

JELLYBEANS

Unlike deer, which shed their antlers every spring, desert bighorn sheep keep their horns, which grow bigger each year.

"Are these bighorn sheep tracks?" Michael asked.

"Yes!" said Mom. "See how they're split? They have hooves with two parts."

Emily asked, "What are these little marks?"

DEW
CLAW

"Those are from its dew claws," said Dad. "They're little claws behind the hoof. Dew claws sometimes show in bighorn sheep tracks in soft ground. Lots of other animals have dew claws, too, including cats and dogs."

"Hey, I think I found another coyote track," said Michael.

"Well, it looks a lot like a coyote track," said Dad. "But look closely. You can see that it doesn't show any claw marks, and the front of the big pad looks dented in."

COYOTE TRACKS

BOBCAT TRACKS

"It's a bobcat track," said Mom.

the STRAIGHT POOP

Since cats can retract their claws, their tracks don't show claw marks. Members of the dog family can't retract their claws, so their tracks do show claw marks—except one: the gray fox. Its claws are so small and sharp that it can climb trees like a cat.

MOUNTAIN
LION

BOBCAT

"Here's another track just like it over here," said Michael. "But this one is *huge*."

"That's because the cat that made it is a lot bigger," replied Mom. "You found your mountain lion."

"Oh, no! Where?" Michael gasped.

"Sorry," said Mom. "I meant you found mountain lion *sign*."

40

"Let's see what you kids learned today," said Dad. "What can you figure out about this mountain lion?"

"I see a bunch of scratch marks on this tree," said Emily. "I think it used it like a scratching post to sharpen its claws!"

the STRAIGHT POOP

Mountain lions have different names in different parts of the country. They're also called panthers, painters, cougars, pumas, and catamounts.

41

"Is this mountain lion scat?" asked Michael.

"It sure is," said Dad. "See how it tried to bury the scat?

"Yeah, and it has bits of hair in it, just like the coyote scat," Michael pointed out.
"They definitely eat other animals."

the STRAIGHT POOP

The mountain lion may be the biggest cat in America, but it still buries its scat just like a housecat.

Emily laid her hand next to the track. "This cat's awfully big," she said.

"That's right," Mom said. "A mountain lion weighs as much as I do, and a big one can weigh more than Dad!"

As the family ate their dinner that night around the campfire, everyone talked about how much fun they had.

"We didn't see very many animals," said Emily, "but it seemed like we did!"

44

Everyone laughed when Michael said,
"And I didn't get scared once!"

TRACKS and SCAT NOTES

BLACK-TAILED JACKRABBIT	BURRO	COYOTE	DESERT BIGHORN SHEEP	DESERT TORTOISE

Small tracks are filled in between the toes.	Tracks are much bigger than deer tracks, and not split.	Tracks are like a dog's, with four toes, usually with visible claw marks.	Pointy split-hoof tracks.	Tracks are basically just round dents with sand or dirt heaped up behind.

The scat is in little balls.	Scat is in chunks, with roughage from vegetation often visible.	Scat is very dark colored with tapered ends and usually contains hair.	Scat is long and oval-shaped like jellybeans, not round like a rabbit's.	Scat is basically cigar-shaped, up to 3 inches long, often with stems and bits of grass in it.

GREAT HORNED OWL	MOJAVE GREEN RATTLESNAKE	MOUNTAIN LION	NORTHERN FLICKER	PACK RAT

GREAT HORNED OWL

Tracks show four toes: two pointing forward and two back or sideways.

Scat is runny and white. "Cough pellets" contain fur and bones.

MOJAVE GREEN RATTLESNAKE

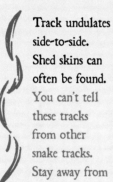

Track undulates side-to-side. Shed skins can often be found. You can't tell these tracks from other snake tracks. Stay away from rattlesnakes.

Scat is long and stringy.

MOUNTAIN LION

Tracks are bigger than a coyote's, but claws don't show.

Scat is rarely seen because they bury it.

NORTHERN FLICKER

Tracks much narrower than owl tracks, with skinny toes pointing almost straight back.

Scat is in long cords.

PACK RAT

Four distinct toes on front feet and five on back feet. Tracks can be about a foot apart when bounding.

Scat is in ovals, smaller around than jackrabbit scat, but longer.

47

ABOUT the AUTHOR and ILLUSTRATOR

GARY ROBSON lives on a ranch near Yellowstone Park in Montana. He received his teaching credential in 1987 and has taught in California and Montana colleges.

He is an expert in closed captioning technology for deaf and hard-of-hearing people. Gary has written fifteen books, ten of them in this series. He and his wife own an independent bookstore in Red Lodge, Montana.

ROBERT RATH is a book designer and illustrator living in Bozeman, Montana. Although he has worked with Scholastic Books, Lucasfilm, and Montana State University, his favorite project is keeping up with his family.

OTHER BOOKS IN THE WHO POOPED IN THE PARK?™ SERIES:

Acadia National Park

Glacier National Park

Grand Canyon National Park

Grand Teton National Park

Great Smoky Mountain National Park

Olympic National Park

Rocky Mountain National Park

Sequoia / Kings Canyon National Parks

Shenandoah National Park

Yellowstone National Park

Yosemite National Park